Pterosaurs
RULERS OF THE SKIES IN THE DINOSAUR AGE

by CAROLINE ARNOLD

Illustrated by LAURIE CAPLE

CLARION BOOKS/New York

For Uno Sjöblom & Ann-Lis Tåg
and all my family across the sea
—L.C.

The author and illustrator would like to thank Dr. Kevin Padian, Professor of Integrative Biology and Curator of the Museum of Paleontology, the University of California, Berkeley, for his expert advice and careful reading of the manuscript.

Clarion Books
a Houghton Mifflin Company imprint
215 Park Avenue South, New York, NY 10003
Text copyright © 2004 by Caroline Arnold
Illustrations copyright © 2004 by Laurie Caple

The illustrations were executed in watercolor.
The text was set in 13-point Hiroshige.

www.houghtonmifflinbooks.com

Printed in Singapore.

Library of Congress Cataloging-in-Publication Data
Arnold, Caroline.
Pterosaurs : rulers of the skies in the dinosaur age / by Caroline Arnold ; illustrated by Laurie Caple.
v. cm.
Includes index.
Contents: Wing lizards—The age of reptiles—The first pterosaurs—The "wing fingers"—Bodies built for flight—Mealtime for pterosaurs—Baby pterosaurs—Discovering pterosaur fossils—Pterodactyl—A Jurassic lagoon—In the air over western Kansas—The Brazilian pterosaurs—A "hairy" pterosaur—The last of the pterosaurs—Where you can see pterosaur fossils.
ISBN 0-618-31354-0
1. Pterosauria—Juvenile literature. [1. Pterosaurs. 2. Prehistoric animals.] I. Caple, Laurie A, ill. II. Title.
QE862.P7A76 2004
567.918—dc22   2003027698

ISBN-13: 978-0-618-31354-9 ISBN-10: 0-618-31354-0

TWP 10 9 8 7 6 5 4 3 2 1

Pterosaur illustrated on title page: *Pteranodon sternbergi.*

Contents

Quetzalcoatlus

Wing Lizards

More than sixty-five million years ago, huge flying reptiles with nearly 40-foot wingspans flew in the skies over what is now southern Texas. Like living sailplanes, they soared on narrow, skin-covered wings, circling on rising air currents, much as eagles and vultures do today. Scientists have given these ancient animals the name *Quetzalcoatlus* (KET-sahl-koh-AHT-lus) after Quetzalcoatl, the winged serpent god of the Aztecs. They are the biggest living creatures ever known to fly.

Quetzalcoatlus belongs to a large and diverse group of flying reptiles called pterosaurs (TARE-oh-sawrs), a name that comes from Greek words meaning "wing lizards." (The *p* in the word *ptero* is not pronounced.) Ranging in size from that of a sparrow to that of a small fighter jet, pterosaurs lived throughout the prehistoric world. Some of them flew over oceans and lakes, scooping up fish from the surface of the water in their long-toothed beaks. Others lived on land, feeding on insects and other food, able to grasp objects with the three clawed fingers at the edge of each of their wings. More than a hundred species of these ancient reptiles are known to have existed, and the list is growing as scientists continue to unearth pterosaur fossils in Brazil, China, Antarctica, and elsewhere. Recent discoveries have revealed new information about pterosaurs and are helping to answer questions about what the world was like when these amazing flying reptiles were alive.

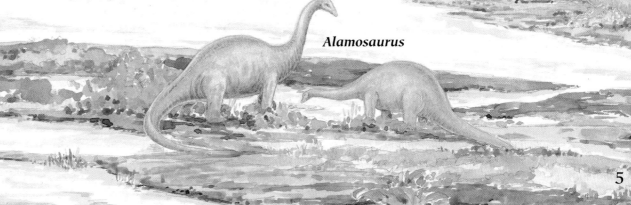

Alamosaurus

The Age of Reptiles

Pterosaurs lived during the Mesozoic Era, a time when Earth's climate was warmer than it is today, the seasons were mild, and there was no ice at the poles. Scientists divide this era into three periods: the Triassic, about 250–208 million years ago; the Jurassic, about 208–144 million years ago; and the Cretaceous, about 144–65 million years ago. The first pterosaurs appeared in the Triassic period, about the same time as the first dinosaurs and the first mammals, and became extinct at the end of the Cretaceous.

The Mesozoic Era is sometimes called the Age of Reptiles because these animals were the dominant life form on Earth then. Dinosaurs walked on the land, huge sea reptiles swam in the oceans, and pterosaurs ruled the skies. Pterosaurs are closely related to dinosaurs and had a common ancestor. Like all other reptiles except turtles, pterosaurs and dinosaurs share certain skeletal features, including two holes in the upper part of the skull and two holes behind the eyes.

One of the oldest known pterosaurs is *Eudimorphodon* (yoo-die-MOR-fo-don), whose name means "true two-form tooth." Its fossil bones, which were first discovered in northern Italy in 1973, are about 215 million years old. *Eudimorphodon* had a wingspan of about 3.3 feet (1 meter) and an unusual arrangement of teeth in its jaws. At the front were several large fangs, and along the sides were rows of smaller teeth, with two more fangs in the middle. Such teeth would have been good for catching and holding fish. Skeletons have been found with fossils of scales in the area of the stomach, indicating that fish were part of this pterosaur's diet.

Eudimorphodon

First pterosaurs
225

Pterosaurs became extinct
65

150

125 *Pterodactyloids*

Basal Pterosauria

250

208

144

65

Millions
of years
ago
300

TRIASSIC

JURASSIC

CRETACEOUS

200

100

Present

M E S O Z O I C   E R A

THE FIRST PTEROSAURS

Scientists classify pterosaurs in two groups according to distinctive features of their skeletons. The early pterosaurs form one group. These pterosaurs typically had long heads, short necks, long, narrow wings, and slender tails that ended in a kind of small sail, which was probably used like a rudder for stability while flying. They were relatively small, ranging in size from that of a robin to that of a large seagull, and they lived between 225 and 125 million years ago. Scientists used to call this group of early pterosaurs the rhamphorhynchoids (RAM-for-RING-koydz), or "prow-beaks," but this term is no longer used. Instead, scientists now call them the basal Pterosauria, a term indicating that they were the original type of pterosaur from which later types evolved. Nearly two dozen species of basal Pterosauria are known. Their fossils have been found in Italy, Germany, England, India, Kazakhstan, Tanzania, Mexico, the United States, and Antarctica.

Dimorphodon

8

A typical early pterosaur was *Dimorphodon* (die-MOR-fo-don) or "two-form tooth." This flying reptile lived about 200 million years ago. It had a rounded jaw with long sharp teeth in front and tiny teeth in back, and it probably ate fish. *Dimorphodon* was about 3.3 feet (1 meter) long and had a wingspan of 4.6 feet (1.4 meters). Its long tail was made up of more than thirty vertebrae and ended in a diamond-shaped sail. *Dimorphodon* was the first pterosaur found in England. The fossil was excavated by Mary Anning in 1828 near her home in Lyme Regis on the Dorset coast. Mary Anning's most famous fossil find was the skeleton of a huge marine reptile, which she discovered in 1812, when she was only twelve years old.

THE "WING FINGERS"

The second group of pterosaurs is called the pterodactyloids (TARE-oh-DAK-ti-loydz), or "wing fingers." They are named after *Pterodactylus* (TARE-oh-DAK-til-us), the first member of the group to be discovered. The pterodactyloids appeared about 150 million years ago. They were the descendants of the early pterosaurs, and in some ways they can be thought of as the "new, improved" models. Many of the new species were highly specialized, and the changes in their body design suggest that they were better than their ancestors at maneuvering in the air. Their heads were longer and narrower than those of the early pterosaurs, and they had extremely short tails. The bones of their hands were larger, and they no longer had a fifth toe.

Pterodactylus kochi

Dsungaripterus weii

The pterodactyloids were a diverse group, with a wide variety of sizes and adaptations. Some, like *Pterodactylus,* whose wingspan ranged from about 14 inches (36 centimeters) to 98 inches (250 centimeters), were fairly small; others, like *Quetzalcoatlus* and its relatives, were enormous. Despite its huge size, *Quetzalcoatlus* weighed only about 110 pounds (50 kilograms). *Dsungaripterus* (jung-gah-RIP-ter-us) was a pterodactyloid that lived about 150–115 million years ago. It had a wingspan of about 10 feet (3 meters). Its name means "Junggar-wing," after the Junggar basin in northwest China, where it was found.

The larger pterosaurs depended on soaring while in the air, but the smaller species were adept at flying fast and changing direction quickly. Like present-day birds and bats, pterosaurs could flap their wings as they maneuvered in the air. The pterodactyloids coexisted with the earlier type of pterosaurs for about thirty million years, until all of the basal Pterosauria species became extinct. The pterodactyloids lived on to the end of the Cretaceous period, when they, too, died out.

Bodies Built for Flight

Pterosaurs were well adapted to life in the air. With hollow, thin-walled bones, their bodies were extremely light. Long wings helped lift them into the skies. Large brains and good vision helped them navigate and maneuver while flying.

Fossil impressions of pterosaur wings show that they were made of a thin skin, or membrane, that formed a web between the bones. Tiny parallel fibers embedded in the skin stiffened the wings for flying. When the pterosaur landed, it folded its wings, making the fibers come together like the spokes of a closed umbrella.

wing fibers magnified

A pterosaur's wing was supported by the bones of the arm and hand. The greatly elongated fourth finger formed the front edge of the wing. If your arms were built like the wings of a pterosaur, your little finger would be more than 3 feet (1 meter) long! Pterosaur skeletons contain a unique structure not found in other reptiles. It is called the pteroid bone. This long bone supported the membrane that connected the wrist to the shoulder and provided a larger wing surface for flight. The first three fingers of the pterosaur's hand extended from the top of the wing, and they could be used to grip rocks or tree trunks while climbing or walking.

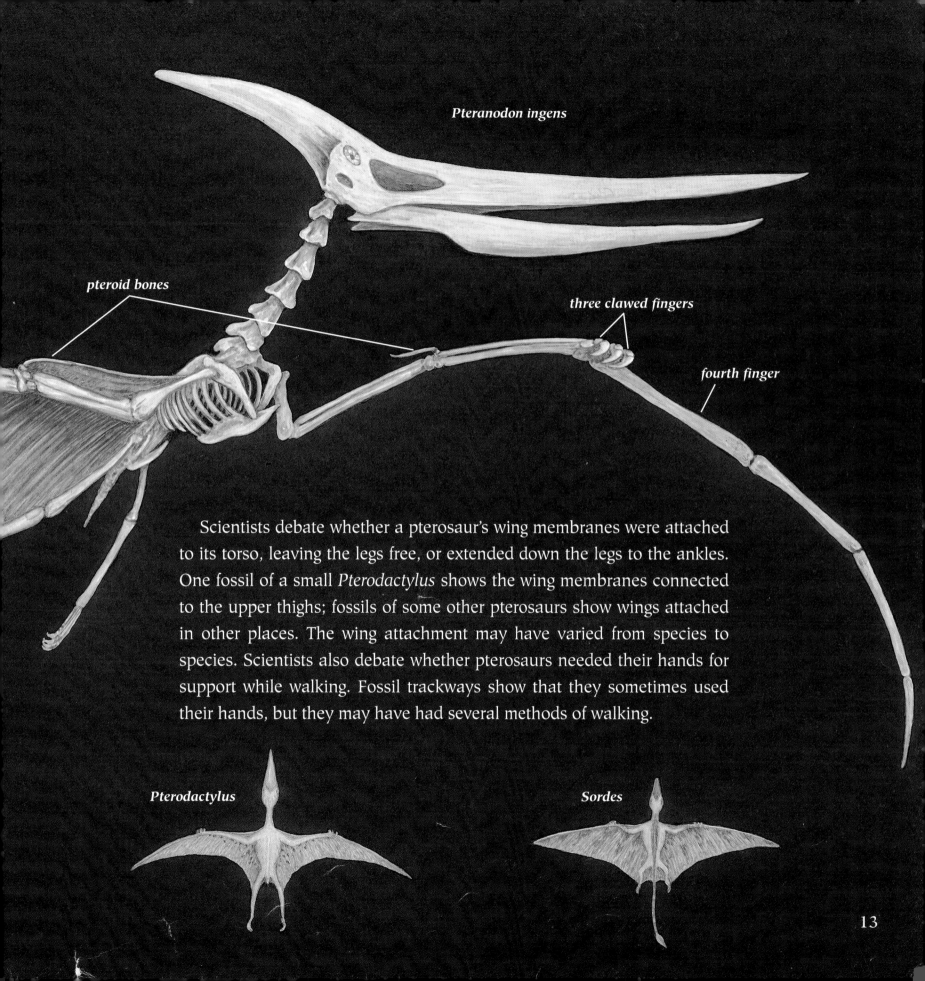

Pteranodon ingens

pteroid bones

three clawed fingers

fourth finger

Scientists debate whether a pterosaur's wing membranes were attached to its torso, leaving the legs free, or extended down the legs to the ankles. One fossil of a small *Pterodactylus* shows the wing membranes connected to the upper thighs; fossils of some other pterosaurs show wings attached in other places. The wing attachment may have varied from species to species. Scientists also debate whether pterosaurs needed their hands for support while walking. Fossil trackways show that they sometimes used their hands, but they may have had several methods of walking.

Pterodactylus

Sordes

13

Mealtime for Pterosaurs

Scientists can learn about the diets of prehistoric animals by examining the shape of their teeth. They can also look at the types of rocks in which the fossils were found in order to find clues to the environment in which the animal lived. In some cases, they can identify the remains of food preserved in the area of the animal's stomach. Like the majority of other reptiles, most pterosaurs were carnivores, or meat eaters. They ate fish, mollusks, crabs, plankton, and insects. They may have also scavenged meat from dead animals. Some pterosaurs may have eaten fruit.

Each species of pterosaur had teeth and jaws adapted to its particular diet. *Quetzalcoatlus* may have used its long, narrow jaws like tweezers or chopsticks to pick up pieces of food from the mud flats where it lived. *Dsungaripterus* had a long, narrow curved jaw and flat teeth at the back of its mouth that would have been good for crushing shells. A species called *Tapejara* (tah-pay-ZHAHR-a), a crested pterosaur recently discovered in Brazil, may have plucked fruits and nuts from tree branches with its thick, toothless beak. *Tapejara* was a small pterosaur, with a skull only 7.9 inches (20 centimeters) long. Its name, which means "old being," comes from the language of the Tupi Indians in Brazil.

Tapejara imperator

15

One of the most specialized adaptations for eating was that of *Pterodaustro* (TARE-oh-DAW-stroh), or "south wing," whose fossil remains have been found in central Argentina. *Pterodaustro* had hundreds of long wire-like teeth lined up along its upwardly curved lower jaw. Scientists think that *Pterodaustro* waded at the edges of lakes and streams, sweeping its bill from side to side in the shallow water, using its teeth as a kind of net or basket to catch tiny pieces of food. Large numbers of *Pterodaustro* fossils have been found in the same place, which suggests that this species flocked together to feed, much as flamingos do today. *Pterodaustro* had a wingspan of 52 inches (1.3 meters). Its skull was 9.3 inches (24 centimeters) long.

Piatnitzkysaurus

Pterodaustro

Baby Pterosaurs

Like most other reptiles, baby pterosaurs probably hatched from eggs. Although fossil eggs known to be from pterosaurs have not yet been found, there are numerous examples of young pterosaurs. One of the smallest is a *Pterodactylus* with a torso length of only .75 inch (2 centimeters) and a wingspan of 7 inches (18 centimeters). It was probably just a few weeks old when it died. Young pterosaurs had fewer and smaller teeth than adults. Their bones also had lots of blood vessels, which carried nutrients to the growing bone. Pterosaurs grew quickly, not like the typical reptiles of today.

Newly hatched pterosaurs would have been too small to care for themselves. Most likely they stayed in their nests, waiting for a parent to bring them food. An intriguing find in Chile suggests that some pterosaurs may have nested in huge colonies, much as seabirds do today. While surveying rock formations in the northern Andes in 1995, scientists found a huge jumble of thousands of pterosaur bones, most of them belonging to young animals. They think that a flash flood may have swept away a nesting colony at one end of a valley and deposited it on the other side. The lack of bones from older pterosaurs suggests that they escaped, while the young pterosaurs, who were not yet able to fly, perished in their nests.

Pterodactylus kochi

19

Discovering Pterosaur Fossils

Fossils of pterosaurs are rarer than those of land-dwelling reptiles because their delicate bones were more easily crushed or broken before they could fossilize. Remains of soft body parts are even rarer because they usually decayed before they could be preserved. Most pterosaur fossils have been found at the edges of prehistoric oceans or lakes, where the remains of dead animals were quickly buried in the soft sediments and thus protected from damage.

Pterosaurs died from a variety of causes, including disease, accidents, natural disasters such as storms and floods, and encounters with other animals. The ability to fly would have allowed pterosaurs to escape from most predators. Nevertheless, fossil bones of pterosaurs with dinosaur teeth embedded in them suggest that pterosaurs sometimes came into conflict with meat-eating dinosaurs. Other fossils reveal that pterosaurs were occasionally eaten by large fish or other ocean predators.

Places where pterosaur fossils have been found

- *Pterodactyloids*
- *Basal Pterosauria*

Rhamphorhynchus

Liopleurodon

Since many pterosaurs lived near water, it is likely that they were able to swim. Fossils of pterosaur feet with the impression of webs between the toes indicate that some species could paddle in the water, much as ducks and other waterbirds do today.

Fossils of pterosaurs have been found on every continent of the world and in diverse locations. The fossils range from single bones to complete skeletons—and even impressions of skin and internal organs. A flurry of pterosaur discoveries in the last thirty years is helping to provide a clearer picture of the appearance and lifestyle of these reptiles. Even so, there are many unanswered questions and conflicting interpretations of the evidence. Each new discovery helps resolve some of these issues—but often raises new questions.

PTERODACTYL

A little more than 200 years ago, workers at a limestone quarry in southern Germany split open a slab and discovered the skeleton of a small reptile embedded in the stone. Although they had come across fossils before, no one had ever seen anything like this one. It had a long toothed beak, a curved neck, and an extremely long finger on each hand. The fossil was placed in the natural history collection at the palace in Mannheim. When the Italian scientist Cosimo Collini catalogued the collection and described the skeleton in 1784, he had no idea what sort of animal could have left these remains. It was not until 1809, when the French anatomist Georges Cuvier saw a drawing of it and realized that the long finger bone was part of the animal's wing, that it was recognized as a flying reptile. Cuvier gave it the name "Pterodactyle" (TARE-oh-DAK-til), or "wing finger," based on the Greek words meaning wing and finger. (Most scientific names are based on Latin or Greek words.) In 1815 the spelling was changed to its present form: pterodactyl. It was the first known fossil of a flying reptile.

Pterodactyl fossils have been discovered in Germany, France, England, North America, and Africa. They represent more than a dozen related species. The species identified by Cuvier is called *Pterodactylus antiquus* (TARE-oh-DAK-til-us an-TIK-wus), or "old wing finger." It lived around 150 million years ago.

A JURASSIC LAGOON

The limestone quarries of southern Germany are one of the world's richest sources of pterosaur fossils. One hundred and fifty million years ago this region was covered by a shallow, warm sea. The quiet waters and fine sediments were ideal for preserving plants and animals that fell to the sea bottom. Fossils of more than fifty species, including fish, insects, pterosaurs, small dinosaurs, and the oldest known birds, have been identified from these deposits. Fossils are so abundant here that it is possible to picture a whole Jurassic environment. Both early, or basal, pterosaurs and their descendants, the pterodactyloids, are buried in the limestone, which shows that the two groups of pterosaurs coexisted.

The most common pterosaur found here is *Rhamphorhynchus* (ram-fo-RING-kus.) This early pterosaur had a long, thin snout with thin pointed teeth. It may have caught fish by spearing them as it flew over the surface of the water. One fossil has the remains of a small fish in its stomach.

Archaeopteryx

Pterodactylus

Compsognathus

Rhamphorhynchus

25

Hundreds of pterosaur fossils representing seventeen species have been excavated in the quarries. *Anurognathus* (a-noor-og-NAY-thus), or "tail-less jaw," had peg-like teeth, which would have been good for eating insects such as wood wasps. *Scaphognathus* (ska-fog-NA-thus), or "tub jaw," was a long-tailed pterosaur and may also have been an insect eater. *German-odactylus* (jer-man-oh-DAK-til-us), or "German finger," was distinguished by a small bony crest and sharp front teeth. *Ctenochasma* (TEEN-oh-KAS-ma), or "comb jaw," had bristle-like teeth, which may have been used as a filter while feeding in the water.

Scaphognathus

Anurognathus

Germanodactylus

Ctenochasma

27

In the Air over Western Kansas

Pterosaur fossils were first discovered in North America in 1870 in the Niobrara chalk cliffs of western Kansas. They belonged to a crested pterosaur named *Pteranodon* (tay-RAN-oh-don), or "toothless wing," which lived at the edge of a large inland sea in the late Cretaceous period. Some *Pteranodon* fossils have been found at least 100 miles (160 kilometers) from the ancient shore, indicating that these reptiles were excellent flyers.

Pteranodon sternbergi had a skull 3.9 feet (1.2 meters) long and a wing-span of about 30 feet (9 meters). This fish eater probably had a throat sac similar to that of a pelican. It lived alongside waterbirds such as *Hesperornis* (hes-per-OR-nis) and *Ichthyornis* (ick-thee-OR-nis), whose fossil bones have also been discovered in the Niobrara chalk deposits.

Scientists are interested in finding out why *Pteranodon* and so many other pterosaurs had crests. Possibly they used the crests as rudders to help them steer and balance while flying. Or the crests may have simply helped the species tell one another apart.

More than a thousand *Pteranodon* fossils have been excavated from the Niobrara chalk. One scientist divided the fossils into two groups by size. He noticed that the smaller animals had wider hips, which would have been better for laying eggs, so it seemed likely that these were females. He also noticed that the smaller *Pteranodon* had relatively small crests, while the larger *Pteranodon* had huge ones. If the larger pterosaurs were males, it may be that bigger crests made them more attractive to females or more impressive to other males. We can imagine that during the mating season the male pterosaurs competed with each other, displaying their large crests in hopes of winning a female's attention in the same way that a male peacock spreads its tail to attract a female today.

Ichthyornis

Pteranodon sternbergi

Hesperornis

29

THE BRAZILIAN PTEROSAURS

Some of the most exciting new discoveries of pterosaurs are being made in northeastern Brazil. These include one species with a 15-foot (4.6-meter) wingspan and a 31-inch (79-centimeter) crest. It is called *Thalassodromeus sethi* (thuh-lass-oh-DRO-mee-us SETH-ee), or "sea runner," after its probable method of capturing prey. Scientists think that this pterosaur skimmed over the surface of the ocean and used its long scissor-like bill to snatch fish from the water.

"Sea runner" is one of more than twenty species of pterosaurs that have been discovered in the rocks at the edge of the Araripe Plateau, about 300 miles (500 kilometers) west of the port city of Recife. In the early Cretaceous, this was the edge of a large ocean. As sediments accumulated near the shore, they buried the remains of countless fish, pterosaurs, and other animals that had lived in or near the water. Over time, these layers became a 650-foot- (200-meter-) thick slab of limestone known as the Santana formation. Pterosaurs from this area are about 110 million years old. The fossils are so well preserved that it is possible in some cases to see how the bones of a skeleton would have actually fit together when the animal was alive. With most other fossils, the skeletons are crushed flat and have to be reconstructed in three dimensions.

Thalassodromeus sethi

Pterosaurs found on the Araripe Plateau include *Anhanguera* (ahn-yahn-GWER-a), or "old devil," and *Tupuxuara* (too-poo-SHWAHR-a), or "familiar spirit." These names come from the language of the local Tupi Indians. Each of these pterosaurs had a crested beak. Another species, *Tropeognathus* (TROPE-ee-og-NAY-thus), or "keel jaw," had a crest on both the top and bottom of its toothed snout. It may have used the bottom crest like the keel on a boat to steady itself as it dragged its mouth through the surface of the water while searching for fish.

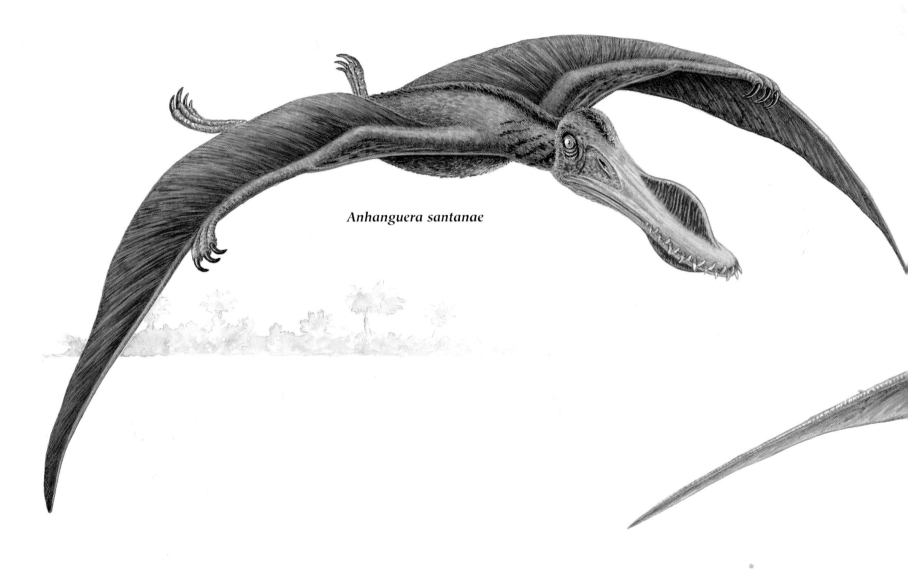

Anhanguera santanae

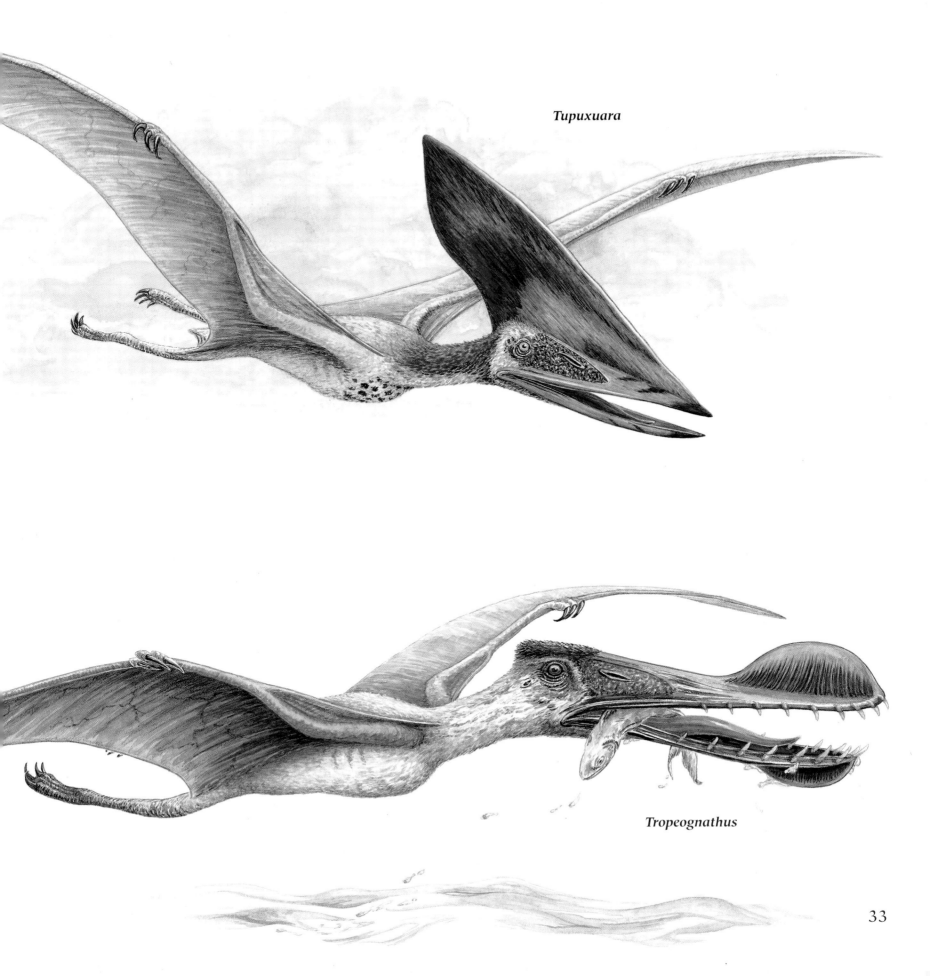

Tupuxuara

Tropeognathus

33

A "Hairy" Pterosaur

Limestone deposits in the Karatau Mountains in Kazakhstan in central Asia are another source of well-preserved pterosaur fossils. In the 1960s, scientists excavated the remains of a small long-tailed pterosaur. There was a nearly complete skeleton, as well as imprints of the soft parts of the body and wings. The most exciting part of this discovery was that there were also imprints of short dense fibers that looked like hair. Because of its apparent furry coat, this pterosaur was named *Sordes pilosus* (SOR-deez pi-LOH-sus), or "hairy evil spirit." Further study of the fossil has shown that the wing fibers probably were not fur but rather structures that helped reinforce the wing membrane. However, it does appear that parts of the body did have short hairlike fibers. A few fossils of other pterosaurs also show traces of hair. Because hair would have helped a pterosaur keep warm and control its body temperature, these discoveries suggest that pterosaurs were warm-blooded animals, unlike today's reptiles. Their rapid growth rate also supports this idea.

Sordes pilosus lived about 150 million years ago and had a wingspan of about 2 feet (63 centimeters). The fossil impression of its wing membranes suggests not only that they were attached to the pterosaur's hind legs but that there was another membrane between the legs. Whether these were the actual positions of the membranes when the pterosaur was alive, or just a result of the animal being flattened during fossilization, is a question scientists continue to debate.

Sordes pilosus

The Last of the Pterosaurs

Pterosaurs were the only reptiles ever capable of powered flight. Although some lizards and snakes can glide through the air, none have the ability to stay aloft, let alone flap. Birds and bats are the only other groups of vertebrates (animals with bony skeletons) that have the ability to fly. Birds first appeared 150 million years ago, at the end of the Jurassic period. They shared the skies with pterosaurs until the end of the Mesozoic Era. Birds are descended from small carnivorous dinosaurs and share a distant ancestor with pterosaurs, but they are not closely related to them. Bats are mammals and are not related to birds or pterosaurs. The oldest known bat lived about 50 million years ago, long after pterosaurs became extinct.

Beginning eighty-eight million years ago, the number of pterosaurs began to diminish. Possible reasons for their gradual disappearance include: increasing competition from birds, a changing climate, or a changing environment. No one knows. But we do know that most of the pterosaurs still around at the end of the Mesozoic were the huge soaring species like *Quetzalcoatlus*. These last pterosaurs became extinct sixty-five million years ago, along with the dinosaurs and many other species.

Pterosaurs were a highly successful group of animals that dominated the skies for most of the dinosaur age. For nearly 150 million years they swooped and dived after fish in the oceans, waded along the shallow shores, and chased insects and perched in trees at the water's edge. Scientists still have many unanswered questions about pterosaurs, but as fossils continue to be discovered, we are learning more about these amazing flying reptiles and their unique place in the Mesozoic world.

Quetzalcoatlus

Where You Can See Pterosaur Fossils

Pterosaur fossils are displayed in many museums. Here are some of the places in North America where you can see and learn about pterosaurs:

The United States

Academy of Natural Sciences, Philadelphia, Pennsylvania

American Museum of Natural History, New York, New York

Carnegie Museum of Natural History, Pittsburgh, Pennsylvania

Denver Museum of Nature and Science, Denver, Colorado

Field Museum, Chicago, Illinois

Museum of Comparative Zoology, Harvard University, Cambridge, Massachusetts

Museum of Paleontology, University of California, Berkeley, California

Museum of the Rockies, Montana State University, Bozeman, Montana

National Museum of Natural History, Smithsonian Institution, Washington, D.C.

New Mexico Museum of Natural History and Science, Albuquerque, New Mexico

Peabody Museum of Natural History, Yale University, New Haven, Connecticut

Sternberg Museum of Natural History, Fort Hays State University, Fort Hays, Kansas

Texas Memorial Museum, University of Texas, Austin, Texas

University of Kansas Natural History Museum, Lawrence, Kansas

Utah Museum of Natural History, Salt Lake City, Utah

Canada

National Museum of Natural Sciences, Ottawa, Ontario

Royal Ontario Museum, Toronto, Ontario

Royal Tyrrell Museum of Paleontology, Drumheller, Alberta

Index

Illustrations of animals other than pterosaurs: birds—*Archaeopteryx*, p. 24, *Hesperornis*, pp. 28–29; *Ichthyornis*, pp. 28–29; dinosaurs—*Alamosaurus*, p. 5, *Piatnitzkysaurus*, p. 16, *Compsognathus*, p. 25; lizard, p. 25; sea reptiles—elasmosaur, p. 6, *Liopleurodon*, p. 21.